TWELVE WERE CHOSEN
A STUDY OF THE ORIGINAL APOSTLES

DAVID LATON, D.MIN.

BibleTalk Books
14998 E. Reno
Choctaw, OK 73020

Copyright © 2021 by BibleTalk.tv
ISBN: 978-1-945778-94-0

Unless specified otherwise, all quotes are from the English Standard Version (ESV).

The Holy Bible, English Standard Version. ESV® Text Edition: 2016. Copyright © 2001 by Crossway Bibles, a publishing ministry of Good News Publishers.

TABLE OF CONTENTS

1. Introduction to The Apostles	5
2. Peter	23
3. Andrew	37
4 James and John	47
5. Philip and Nathanael	57
6. Matthew and Thomas	69
7. James the Less, Simon the Zealot, and Judas Not Iscariot	83
8. Judas Iscariot	93
9. Matthias and Paul	103
10. Faith	115

1.
Introduction to The Apostles

Not long after Jesus began His earthly ministry and as the crowds following Him began to grow, He called out twelve men and designated them as apostles. From our view, there was nothing extraordinary about these men. Some have described these men as extraordinary in their ordinariness. They were not selected because of their social status, education, religious, or political connections. They were simply ordinary people, just like us.

Our Lord knew the wealth of raw materials possessed by each of these men. He knew what they could become. Except for Judas Iscariot, the one who betrayed Him, they learned to turn their lives over to Him.

That is the overall message for us. We can do extraordinary things for the Master as we learn to turn our lives over to Him. Each of us has been gifted by God to turn what we might think of as ordinary into the extraordinary. The extraordinary things we do involve showing Jesus to others and helping them enter into a relationship with Him. That is a critical task for us as disciples. And just like these men, we learn that the power is not in us, but in God and seen through us as we each turn more and more of our lives over to Him.

In Acts 2:42-47 we see the early actions of the church just after it had been established on Pentecost Sunday. Of special note is the statement in verse 42:

> "And they devoted themselves to the apostles' teaching..." *They took ownership of what was taught to them.*

We continue today to dedicate our lives to our Lord and apply the apostles' teachings. In this series of lessons, we are going to look at these men. We will look at their strengths and weaknesses and what we can learn from each.

Leadership is the ability to lead others. We learn to imitate them.

In this first lesson we will learn:

- The difference between an apostle and a disciple
- Selecting the twelve
- What the apostles had to overcome

The Difference Between Disciple and Apostle

In the gospels the term "disciple" is used to describe both followers of Christ in general and the twelve apostles specifically. A disciple is a common term for someone that is a learner, pupil, student or follower of a specific teacher. It is also used to demonstrate agreement and acceptance of the teacher as leader. Disciples would attach themselves to a teacher, even travel with this teacher for a while. Some of the disciples of Jesus traveled with Him in the region where He was teaching for a time. Others, like the apostles, traveled with Him continually.

Jesus was certainly not the first to have disciples. Discipleship was a common education model of the time. The value in this educational model is that it lends itself to learning by experience. This is where the master, Jesus in this case, was able to apply real-world examples and experiences to help the disciples achieve deeper understanding. Evidence of this is in how Jesus would bring in examples from nature (Matthew 6:25-34) and the many parables where He drew from life experiences and common knowledge to teach deeper truths.

In Matthew 28:18-20, in what is called the "great commission," Jesus told the apostles, and us by extension, to make other disciples (followers) for Him. Our efforts result in disciples, or followers for Christ, not for ourselves.

The word Apostle, on the other hand, means "the sent out" or "the sent ones." An apostle is an official representative speaking with the authority on behalf of the one who sent him. Jesus provided these men with knowledge, additional power, and authority to fulfill their role.

Today, each of us can (must) become a disciple of Jesus, but we cannot become His apostle. These initial twelve, and later Matthias and Paul, were the only ones appointed to this role. There were some people at that time and there are some today who claim to be apostles in the same context. They should heed Paul's warnings:

> "For such men are false apostles, deceitful workmen, disguising themselves as apostles of Christ. And no wonder, for even Satan disguises himself as an angel of light. It is no surprise if his servants, also, disguise themselves as servants of righteousness. Their end will correspond to their deeds."
> - 2 Corinthians 11:13-15

How Jesus Selected the Twelve Apostles

We read the details of how Jesus prepared Himself and selected the Twelve in Mark 3:13 and Luke 6:12. Luke begins with the expression, "In these days." This is like Paul's expression from Galatians 4:4, "But when the fullness of time had come...." This clearly indicates events were on our Lord's timeline and fully under His control. Scholars estimate this occurred approximately two years before His crucifixion so there was a time of Jesus teaching a larger group of disciples and then His focus on the Twelve who would serve as apostles as His ministry progressed.

Luke 6:12 records that Jesus isolated Himself with a prayer to God. Imagine that time for moment. Here is Jesus, the Son of God, praying to the Father, and no doubt in the presence of the Holy Spirit. This would have been a special time seeking the wisdom and assurance through this "inter-Trinitarian communion". This should remind us clearly of our Lord's prayer in John 17 as He prepares Himself for His torture and death (see also Matthew 26:36-44). In this prayer Jesus prays for the apostles specifically, and us as well.

As we see in the record of the calling of the apostles in the gospels (not including John), after a night of prayer Jesus called His disciples together as a group. From that larger group He selects the twelve and names them as apostles. He had already offered some of the men a personal

Matt. 10:1

invitation to follow Him, but up to this point, they were just a part of the larger group of disciples.

It is a good question to ask why Jesus selected twelve. What is significant about that number? Most scholars see this number as symbolic of the twelve tribes of Israel that formed the Jewish nation. It further can symbolize God's new kingdom. Later, as the disciples were waiting for the arrival of the Holy Spirit following the ascension of Jesus, they recognized the importance of this number as they selected Matthias to replace Judas (Acts 1:12-26).

Similarities and Differences

The apostles are listed in the gospels of Matthew, Mark, and Luke, but not in John. John gives us details about the activities and events involving many of the apostles. The apostles are also listed in Acts but obviously do not include Judas Iscariot since he had already taken his life following his betrayal of Jesus.

The listings of the apostles are arranged in three groups of four and in descending order, apparently based on their level of closeness with Jesus. The listing seems to reflect the details, or lack of details of their lives during the ministry of Jesus. This is not to say any were ineffective or insignificant, but reflects the way the gospel writers chose to portray them.

Note also that several of the apostles were known by different names depending on how they are portrayed in the gospels. We will examine this more closely as we review each apostle individually.

Matthew 10:2-4	Mark 3:16-19	Luke 6:12-16	Acts 1:13; 26
Peter Andrew James John	Peter James John Andrew	Peter Andrew James John	Peter John James Andrew
Philip Bartholomew Thomas Matthew	Philip Bartholomew Matthew Thomas	Philip Bartholomew Matthew Thomas	Philip Thomas Bartholomew Matthew
James Thaddeus Simon the Zealot Judas Iscariot	James Thaddeus Simon the Zealot Judas Iscariot	James Simon the Zealot Judas the Son of James Judas Iscariot	James Simon the Zealot Judas - Son of James Matthias (vs. 26)

Group one lists Peter first and includes Andrew, James, and John. They are among the first disciples Jesus called (John 1:35-42) and were with Him at key times. They seem to be the only group with common denominators: two sets of brothers who were all fishermen. There are indicators that some of the other apostles were also fishermen and may have had some familial connections, although Scripture does not clearly show this. Peter, James, and John form an even closer inner circle and were with Jesus at major events such as the Transfiguration and as Jesus prayed at Gethsemane.

Group two has Philip first and includes Bartholomew (named Nathanael in John), Matthew, and Thomas.

Group three is led by James the son of Alphaeus and includes Simon the Zealot; Judas, son of James, and Judas Iscariot. This group, except for Judas Iscariot, is hardly ever mentioned in Scripture. Judas Iscariot always appears last and is identified in some way as the traitor.

We also see significant personality characteristics and occupational differences among the disciples. For example, Matthew was a tax collector, despised by the Jews and Simon was a Zealot, committed to killing Romans and anyone representing them, such as Matthew. Peter was brash, outspoken, and aggressive while John and Andrew spoke little. To restate a significant point about them, these men were not among the elite in their society.

There were no religious or community leaders among them. Some were completely obscure. Some were despised and feared. Some were common workmen struggling to survive. All together, they were ordinary men with the raw materials to serve Jesus, and through Him, change humanity forever.

What is important is not what they were but what they would become. They would become instruments for our Lord accomplishing the extraordinary because they followed the Master as they learned to put Him forward rather than self. That is the lesson for us. In selecting these men from the common, ordinary citizens of the day, Jesus is reflecting His methodology. He taught what was unexpected and dispelled "conventional wisdom". His apostles were perceived as common, unqualified, and unworthy men (Acts 4:13). These men rose to the height of usefulness and effectiveness because they turned their lives over to Jesus.

It's not about us. It's about God working through us!

Their Task

As Jesus selected the Twelve, He delegated His power and authority to them to be able to cast out demons, heal, and proclaim the message of the Messiah's arrival. He selected them, taught them, and then sent them out (Matthew 10:1 and following).

Although Jesus taught many different groups at times, we see that as His ministry continued, and as He approached His ascension to heaven, He increased His focus on the

Twelve to prepare them for their role of carrying the gospel to the world.

In Matthew 16:19 (see also Matthew 18:18) He gave them extraordinary authority that would enable them to fulfill their role of leading His Kingdom. In this passage He states:

> "I will give you the keys to the kingdom of heaven, and whatever you bind on earth shall be bound in heaven, and whatever you loose on earth shall be loosed in heaven."

What the Apostles Had to Overcome

We stated that these men were ordinary people with no specified attributes. They did, however, possess the raw materials that would help them in their role. They also had much to overcome, and much to unlearn. In doing so, they teach us lessons that we can use in our spiritual journey today.

They lacked spiritual understanding

The disciples saw what they had been taught to see. In the Sermon on the Mount (Matthew 5, 6, 7) Jesus used the expression, "You have heard that is was said...but I say...." This was done to point out misunderstandings of God's word and intent. John records that after he and Peter viewed the empty tomb, even they did not understand the Scripture that Jesus must rise from the dead (John 20:9). To overcome this lack of spiritual understanding, Jesus kept teaching them, even after his resurrection and up to the moment of His ascension.

We also lack spiritual understanding at times and may have been taught an incomplete truth or misunderstanding of God's word. Like the apostles, we can learn truth. We have the teachings of Jesus dutifully recorded in the gospels that we learn from thorough study, meditation and prayer. And like the first-century Christians, we have the teaching of the apostles (Acts 2:42) and other writers of the New Testament to guide us.

They lacked humility

At times, the apostles were focused entirely on self in their lack of spiritual maturity. They even argued over who should be first or greatest in the Kingdom while standing in the presence of the Son of God.

Jesus overcame this by teaching and demonstrating humility, even to giving His life for them. He continually taught them humility throughout His ministry. This critical characteristic was even at the heart of His lesson on service on the night of His arrest as He washed their feet. We learn from this that our usefulness to God begins with our humble acceptance of His will and continues as we grow spiritually.

They lacked faith

On several occasions, Jesus said to the apostles, "Oh you of little faith." Jesus kept teaching them and doing miracles to not only show His deity but to increase their faith (John 20:30-31). We must wonder if at later times as they looked upon a flower or observed birds going about their lives, they reflected on or recalled the lessons of the Sermon on the Mount. Perhaps they reflected on His words as they traveled through a storm, climbed a mountain, or saw a tree along the seashore (Matthew 8:26; 17:20; Luke 17:6).

From the teachings and example of Jesus, we learn that faith is the foundation of our relationship with God. As the Hebrews writer states:

> "Without faith, it is impossible to please him, for whoever would draw near to God must believe that he exists and that he rewards those who seek him."
> - Hebrews 11:6

They lacked commitment

Although the apostles remained with Jesus when many of the disciples turned from following him (John 6:66), they would later abandon Him. After Jesus was arrested in the garden of Gethsemane, the disciples as a group fled in fear. Only Peter and John followed, but from a distance. This was after strong statements of their recognition of Jesus as the

Son of God, King of Israel, and claims that they would follow Him even to death. The most memorable moment of their failure is Peter denying Jesus three times, even swearing he did not know Him (Luke 22:54-62).

Jesus overcomes <ins>their lack of commitment by</ins> this by teaching, forgiving and praying for them (John 17:6-19). We all experience periods when our commitment wanes. We return to the teachings of Jesus and the writers of the New Testament to strengthen our faith and sustain our commitment.

They lacked power

We have already noted that these men were ordinary men. On their own, they were weak and helpless. They craved power but misunderstood what true power was and how God wanted them to obtain and use it. Jesus gave them power as His representatives (Matthew 10:1) and later sent the Holy Spirit to empower them on Pentecost Sunday (Acts 2) as promised. They progressed from arguing about being the greatest in the Kingdom to gaining and using power to show Jesus to the world. They would recognize that it was God's power working through them and not their own.

This is an important lesson for us. As we mature spiritually, we seek God's power working in us and continue to grow in our faith and dedication to our Lord. As we are successful in our efforts, we continue to give praise and glory to God.

<ins>Just as the apostles did, we learn to put God's will ahead of ours.</ins>

<ins>We enter into a relationship w/ Jesus upon our baptism + as a result</ins>

of that, we begin to grow spiritually.

How the Apostles Died

Scripture only records the actual death of James (Acts 12:1-2) and Judas Iscariot (Matthew 27:5). In John 21:18-19, John records a statement by Jesus that is believed to indicate Peter would die by crucifixion. However, it is not specifically stated in Scripture how or when he died. In John 21:20-23, Jesus makes a statement regarding John indicating he would live a longer life, as we know he did. John died of natural causes.

Secular, (or non-Biblical history) including the writings of various early Christians, gives us several accounts of how the apostles died. Some of these accounts conflict with one another, bordering on the mythological, and are discounted. Each following chapter addresses some of these traditions and legends. Please remember, as noted, scripture is silent on many of the actions and death of the apostles. The information provided is not necessarily factual.

Perhaps we are asking the question about how they died in the wrong way. It was not their deaths that mattered, but their lives. The correct answer to the question of how they died is this, except Judas Iscariot, these men died faithful to the Lord they came to love, even more than their lives. Their lives and deaths serve as examples of faithfulness for us.

Conclusion

We may wonder why Jesus bothered. The answer is because God loves us and is committed to our salvation through

Jesus (John 3:16-17; 1 John 3:16). We also know that it is through God's power and not our own that He is glorified.

We see these men making the transition from ordinary to extraordinary, unremarkable to remarkable with a clear mission to teach Jesus to all the world. Their transition and success were not from anything they did of themselves, but from what they allowed God to do through them. This was the key to their success; they allowed God to work through them. They did this by doing God's will.

The same happens today. We can do remarkable things for God not through miracles and wonders as the apostles did, and not for ourselves, but by allowing God to work through us as obedient and faithful servants, doing His will and bringing glory to Him. This is a capability we all have that can grow.

As we see in these men, God is more interested in what we can become rather than who and what we are. What He wants is for us to become like His Son, Jesus Christ. Becoming more Christlike begins with our obedient response of faith as we repent and are baptized (Acts 2:38) and continues as we grow in the grace and knowledge of our Lord and Savior Jesus Christ (2 Peter 3:18).

Hopefully, as we progress through this study and grow to become like Jesus, we will give God the glory in all things.

Discussion Questions

1. What is the difference between a disciple of Christ and an apostle?

2. What is significant about Jesus praying before selecting the twelve disciples?

3. What is significant about Jesus selecting twelve apostles?

4. What authority did the apostles have and how does that impact us today? (Matthew 16:19 and Matthew 18:18)

5. How can you use this lesson to grow spiritually and help others come into a relationship with Jesus?

2.
Peter

First Among the Twelve

Some have called Peter, "the apostle with a foot-shaped mouth." Others have called him, "the first rock star." We know that Peter certainly had some interesting characteristics that could be viewed negatively, but there is also a more positive view of Peter. He could be called, "Peter, the apostle who became all he could become."

Many of us associate ourselves closely with Peter because we see in him many of the character traits we possess or wish to possess (or perhaps wish we did not possess). I think this is a positive view since we certainly can follow Peter's example in allowing Jesus to shape him into the man who indeed would become "first" in many ways. It was a journey for Peter that was sometimes filled with exciting moments, sometimes deeply sorrowful moments, even times where he seemed to be coming apart. Yet, although his faith was weakened, Peter never lost faith as he lived his life dedicated to the Master.

What we know of Peter for certain and what is important to our walk of faith is contained in Scripture. There are secular, or non-scriptural writings, that give traditional accounts of Peter's life. Our focus will be on what Scripture records of some of his actions and interactions and what we can learn from this remarkable man.

A Bit About Peter

Peter's original name was Simon Bar-Jonah, or Son of Jonah (or John). In John 1:42, Jesus changes his name to Peter which means "rock." Sometimes we see Peter referred to as, Simon Peter, Simon, or Cephas.

Sometimes Jesus referred to him as Peter, other times Simon, and sometimes by both names. Jesus refers to Peter as Simon as He tells of his upcoming denial of Him (Luke 22:31-34). As Jesus is praying in the garden, He mildly rebukes Peter for sleeping during the time and calls him Simon (Mark 14:32-42). Then, when Peter makes his great confession of faith about Jesus in Matthew 16:16-18, Jesus refers to him as, "Simon-Bar-Jonah" and "Peter". We also see Jesus referring to Peter as, "Simon" as He reinstates him in John 21:15-19. Whatever the name Jesus used, Peter clearly understood he was being personally addressed by our Lord, sometimes in praise, sometimes in rebuke, but always from the frame of reference of truly knowing Peter.

Peter is commonly associated with the villages of Bethsaida and Capernaum. Along with Chorazin (Korazim), these villages were within an area of approximately five miles on the north shore of the Sea of Galilee. Peter worked in this area as a fisherman with his brother Andrew and two others who also became apostles, James and John. Capernaum was also Peter's home and became a hub from where Jesus would travel through the region. Even with the influence of Jesus and Peter, these villages were generally unreceptive towards Jesus and His message (Matthew 11:20-24).

We know little about his family except he had a wife and mother-in-law (Matthew 8:14-15). Jesus heals Peter's mother-in-law, then she got up and served them. The healing was immediate and complete thus demonstrating the power of Jesus.

Many events in the gospels and the book of Acts involve Peter specifically and generally. We will now look at a few events that shaped Peter in became first among the apostles.

Key Events of Peter from Scripture

Peter's Calling

Peter's calling involved a two-step process. First, in John 1 we read where John the Baptist pointed out Jesus to two of his disciples, Andrew and John. They spent the rest of the day with Jesus. Following this, Andrew goes to Peter and exclaims "We have found the Messiah" (John 1:41). Later, in Matthew 4:18-19, we read where Jesus was walking by the Sea of Galilee and called Peter and his brother Andrew to follow him. This marked the beginning of their full-time following of Jesus. Of special note in Matthew's account is that they immediately left their work and followed Him. After the resurrection of Jesus, Peter and some of the others went back to fishing as they continued to deal with the realization that Jesus had risen (John 21:1-3).

Peter Provides the Correct Answer

In Matthew 16 Jesus is with his disciples in the region of Caesarea Philippi. This area was dedicated to idol worship, including a cave turned into a shrine to the Greek god, Pan. This cave was called, "The Gates of Hell". Jesus asked the apostles who people were saying He was. They replied; John the Baptist, Elijah, Jeremiah, or one of the prophets. Jesus then asked a more direct question, who did they think He was. Peter quickly spoke up and stated, "You are the Christ, the Son of the living God." (Matthew 6:15-16)

His reply pleased Christ, who informed him that those words were not his own, but that it was God Himself who had revealed Christ's true identity to him. This response clearly indicates that Peter was developing a deeper awareness and faith into who Jesus was.

At that time Jesus revealed to the apostles a significant insight into His ministry and their role and authority in supporting it. Jesus continued with the statement:

> "...on this rock, I will build my church, and the gates of hell shall not prevail against it. I will give you the keys to the Kingdom of heaven..."
> - Matthew 6:18-19

We know keys lock and unlock. Jesus explains this as He states that what the apostles bind on earth will be bound in heaven and whatever they loosed on earth shall be loosed in heaven. If we put it all together, Jesus is stating that He will soon establish His Kingdom on earth and the false gods and mistaken beliefs of mankind will not withstand the truth of His word. Further, the apostles, and Peter specifically, would be the instrument through which this would occur.

Although Peter provides the answer and facilitates the discussion, these words of binding and loosening were addressed to the apostles as a group. We see evidence of this later as all the apostles would have leading roles in carrying the gospel to the world. But in the role as a leader among the apostles, we see Peter taking the first important steps in carrying out the Lord's directive to take the gospel to all the world. Through his life, Peter was the first to reveal God's plan for our salvation:

- Acts 2 – Pentecost
- Acts 8 – To the Samaritans
- Acts 10 – Converting the first non-Jews

Peter's Denial of Christ and Reinstatement

In Luke 22:31-34, Jesus tells Peter that he will deny him, even as Peter declares he is ready to go to prison or even death with him. Then in Luke 22:54-60 we read how Peter denied he knew Jesus three times, just as Jesus had said he would. In John 21:15-17 we read where Peter is sitting with Jesus after his resurrection. Three times Jesus asks Peter if he loves Him. Peter strongly states he does. The process of asking three times is a reflection of the three times Peter denied our Lord. The event was not lost on Peter as he would spend the rest of his life completely dedicated to Jesus. We will look at these events in detail in a later lesson.

It took a lifetime of growth for Peter to reach his full potential in his service to the Lord. From him, we learn how to reach our potential in the Lord's service.

Peter was a seeker. He had a confident type of courage. He learned humility & compassion.

What We Learn from Peter

We learn to be a seeker.

We see more recorded questions by Peter than from all the other apostles combined. He usually was the one who asked the Lord to explain His difficult parables (Matthew 15:15; Luke 12:41). He not only asked many questions but was also the first who answered questions posed by Christ. Peter would usually speak up while the others were processing the question. He speaks more than the rest, is spoken to by the Lord most often, is the most rebuked by the Lord, and most boldly confesses the Lord. All these behaviors show Peter engaged fully to discover more about our Lord and to grow from that knowledge.

We must seek first to become a follower of Jesus and then continue to seek how we can grow in service to the Lord and how we can better carry out our mission as servants to the Master.

We learn about the courage necessary to fulfill our role.

Being a fisherman carried a high level of danger and required courage. Later Peter changed his natural courage into a mature, settled, and quietly confident and unshakable type of courage where he truly was willing to suffer anything for Christ. One key piece of evidence is that he had the courage to return to our Lord when he realized his failures.

That courage and humility was rewarded by reinstatement by our Lord.

After he delivered the keys to enter into God's Kingdom through the powerful address at Pentecost (Acts 2) we see Peter's re-directed courage as he began to carry the gospel of Christ to the world. There he stands before crowds boldly proclaiming for the first time Jesus, the Savior, and how to gain salvation. Later we see:

- Peter and John speaking courageously before the Sanhedrin – Acts 4

- Peter arrested but continuing to preach Jesus even after being threatened – Acts 5

- Peter taking the Gospel to the Samaritans and Gentiles (non-Jews) and later defending them before the brethren in Jerusalem – Acts 8, 10, 11, 15

The lesson here is, do not hesitate to return to our Lord in repentance and continue courageously to fulfill our mission to bring Jesus to others.

We learn to develop humility.

Peter is clearly shown as confident, self-assured, and aggressive. The events experienced from his calling by Christ, the lessons learned as he traveled and served with our Lord, the failure to keep a watch in the garden, his denial of Christ and his reinstatement all worked to transform Peter's overconfident and aggressive nature resulting in a humble servant giving him the insights to write the following:

> "Humble yourselves, therefore, under the mighty hand of God so that at the proper time he may exalt you..."
> - 1 Peter 5:6

Jesus stated that humility was a blessing as He began the Sermon on the Mount (Matthew 5:3-5). Humility is at the heart of being poor in spirit and meek. Humility is a key characteristic of Christ and those who choose to follow Him. Like Peter, we learn that life is not about us, but about the Master, whom we serve humbly and faithfully.

We learn to be compassionate.

Compassion means to show care for others. Compassion is a characteristic of Jesus, and something Peter would learn as he received compassion when Jesus forgave and reinstated him (John 21:15-19). It was not just theoretical concepts but rather experiential learning that Peter was relying on.

Because of the knowledge of his personal weaknesses and our Lord's forgiveness, Peter was able to teach us that no matter the sin in our lives, we can turn to our Lord and receive that same forgiveness. Once forgiven, we now are armed with the knowledge and strength of our Lord to grow in all ways as a faithful servant. Therefore, we too must develop and grow in compassion if we are to be like Christ. We demonstrate our compassion for others as we, like Peter, show Jesus to all.

Conclusion

Within the book of Acts, we see a clear division between the actions primarily of Peter and those of Paul. This change in the narrative occurs following Peter's rescue from Herod in Acts 12:6-17. Luke ends this narrative stating, "Then he departed and went to another place." We are not certain where that was, but it serves as a change in focus. It is not that Peter did not remain active, but rather Luke changes the narrative to focus on Paul. It is a fair question to wonder what happened to Peter after the church began to spread and he was no longer the focus of Acts.

There is no mention in Scripture of where Peter continued to teach, his death, or his burial. There is strong evidence from the secular writings of historians and early church leaders that Peter was eventually killed by crucifixion in Rome during the reign of Nero around 64 to 66 AD. Tradition holds that he was crucified upside down because he did not want to be crucified in the same manner as Jesus.

Aside from the example of being faithful unto death, Peter's life is of primary importance. He became all that our Lord expected of him because he regained and sustained his focus on obeying and serving Jesus.

Peter is credited with writing two books of the New Testament, I & II Peter. Scholars also believe he influenced Mark's gospel. In 2 Peter 3:18, we see his life summed up in his final recorded words:

> "But grow in the grace and knowledge of our Lord and Savior Jesus Christ. To him be the glory both now and to the day of eternity. Amen."

That is exactly what Peter did, and why he grew to match the essential meaning of his name, "Rock" a foundational figure in the building of our Lord's church (Matthew 16:18).

At the same time, we see a real person who serves as an example of God's power to change ordinary people into useful and productive servants. Just like Peter, all of us desperately need the salvation only Jesus offers.

Peter changed from the one seeking his way to one seeking our Lord's way. He would have loved to sing the old gospel hymn, "Have Thine Own Way Lord." He would especially be fond of the second verse:

"Have thine own way Lord, have Thine own way.
Hold o'er my being absolute sway!
Whiter than snow Lord, wash me just now,
As in Thy presence Humbly I bow."

Discussion Questions

1. What was significant about Peter's response to Jesus in Matthew 16:13-20?

2. Why was Peter reinstated by Jesus after he had denied Him and how does this apply to us? (John 21:15)

3. In what ways was Peter a seeker and what is the example for us?

4. What is your favorite or most impactful event from Peter's life and how does it help you grow spiritually?

5. How can you use this lesson to grow spiritually and help others come into a relationship with Jesus?

3.
Andrew

A Brother Among Brothers

As we introduced this series of lessons on the apostles, we stated that these men gave us lessons we can learn. This is no less true with Andrew. Although there is little in the Scripture about him, he stands out as a wonderful example for us to follow.

As stated, many identify with Peter, but we might have more in common with Andrew. For example, have you ever:

- Encouraged someone with a smile?
- Invited someone to a Bible study?
- Invited someone to church to hear a special speaker?
- Picked up someone to bring them to services?
- Taken food to someone?
- Given someone a book to read or a pamphlet about a specific Bible subject?

These are just a few ways we have shared the characteristics of Andrew. In doing so we have shared the gifts God has given us. Our Lord taught the disciples, and us to use the gifts God has provided us to glorify the Father. This is especially part of the teachings to the apostles in Matthew 25 when our Lord taught about judgment. Starting in verse 14 He taught the great Parable of the Talents, clearly instructing us to use what God has given us for His glory. Then in the final judgment scene described by Jesus notice the focus, feeding others less fortunate, giving a drink to the thirsty, welcoming strangers, clothing the naked, and visiting the sick and imprisoned. Jesus states that when we do this, we are doing it to Him. When we do not do this, we are withholding it from Him (Matthew 25:31-46). This is consistent with our Lord's answer to what is the greatest commandment from Matthew 22:36-40. Andrew and the others would have heard this and learned to put it into practice.

As we are doing with all these lessons, we will focus on the biblical information about Andrew and what we can learn from him. Sometimes our transformation in Christ is drastic. With most of us, however, the transformation is gradual and steady. Like Andrew, we might not notice the change, but as we remain focused and faithful, change will occur.

Biblical Information

Andrew was among the first to become a disciple of Jesus. As Andrew is introduced to us in John 1, we see that he is a disciple of John the Baptist who points Jesus out to Andrew, and apparently to John who will also become a disciple of Jesus. They leave John the Baptist and go with Jesus (John 1:35-40) to spend the afternoon with Him. Imagine the thrill of that afternoon. They would marvel in the discovery of the Christ as they listened to every word of Jesus. It is no wonder that afterwards Andrew immediately went to his brother Peter with the words, "We have found the Messiah!" (John 1:41).

I find it interesting that after Andrew and Peter's first encounter with our Lord as recorded by John, they apparently returned to their fishing. Imagine the conversation between the two brothers after meeting our Lord.

In Matthew's account of the calling of Peter and Andrew to become disciples, we see that the two brothers had returned to their fishing, and when Jesus personally called the two to become fishers of men, they immediately left their nets to become full-time disciples and later apostles (Matthew 4:18-20).

On two occasions Andrew is teamed up with Philip, who also became a disciple, to bring others to Jesus. In John 6:8-11, Jesus fed the 5,000 with the barley loaves and fish brought by a boy. Philip was uncertain how they would feed so many. Andrew apparently noticed the young boy with the meager provisions and asked Jesus how that little would feed so many. Later, in John 12:20-22, Philip again brings two foreigners (Greeks) to Andrew who then introduces them to Jesus.

The last mention we see of Andrew is at the ascension of Jesus in Acts 1:6-11. He, along with the others, strained to capture one more glimpse of the Lord as He returned to heaven.

When compared to Peter, James, and John, we see Andrew has a different personality. Andrew seems to be one who quietly guides others to meet our Lord. Andrew seemed to be pleased to do what he could for our Lord with the gifts he had and supporting others to do likewise.

Of the disciples in the inner circle, Andrew seems to be the most thoughtful. Peter, we know to have been impetuous, rushing ahead, frequently saying the wrong thing at the wrong time. James and John were nicknamed "Sons of Thunder," because of their reckless tendencies (Mark 3:17). Scripture never directly attaches anything negative to Andrew. When Jesus would rebuke, Andrew was included in the group, not singled out individually.

Never see Andrew rebuked by Jesus.

What We Learn from Andrew

Andrew teaches us that every individual is valuable. *He understood the value of the individual.*

We have already stated that when we see Andrew, he is usually bringing someone to Jesus. It does not matter whether it is to learn from Jesus or to deal with a situation, his focus is bringing someone to Jesus. There is no confusion on his part. That should be our focus. Whether by ourselves or teamed with another, we must ask ourselves how we can introduce this person to Jesus.

Along with the value of the individual, we see Andrew knows the value of personal contact.

Personal contact is the strongest form of evangelism. Rarely is someone converted to our Lord from just hearing a Gospel sermon. Usually someone invites the person to come where there is some sort of relationship, study, and contact. Sometimes a person may not even have attended "church" until he or she has been converted.

Andrew was someone's "link in the chain" of events leading to their conversion. It is very possible that at judgment when the faithful are gathered with the Lord, you might see Andrew in your links in the chain of those who influenced you for the Lord.

Andrew teaches us the value of simple gifts.

We might think we have little to offer God or that what we do is not important, but that is from our perspective. Maybe what we offer is only a smile, an invitation or a small kindness performed for one in need. The reality is that God has graced each of us with what we need to serve Him as we can. Never underestimate what God can do with what we have.

Conclusion

As mentioned, there is little within the scripture record of Andrew. Tradition has it that Andrew continued to teach the gospel in what is now Russia. There is also a tradition that Andrew traveled to Asia Minor, modern-day Turkey, and Greece.

Tradition says Andrew was crucified in Greece near Athens on an X shaped cross. One account states that Andrew converted the wife of a Roman governor who had Andrew crucified because she would not recant her faith.

Andrew clearly shows us that the power of greatness is in our Lord. We may feel that we cannot do much or that we do not have great skill or ability to offer our Lord. That is the furthest thing from reality. We all have talents and resources, some unique to us, that we can use to bring others to Christ, just as our brother Andrew did. Through his example we can see that we too can use our gifts to become all that Jesus wants us to become.

Andrew was among the first to hear and follow Jesus. He was part of the inner circle, close to Jesus most of the time and he experienced much of the glory of our Lord. He spent a lifetime doing what he enjoyed the most, bringing others to Jesus.

Andrew would love to sing the old spiritual song, "Balm of Gilead." He would especially have enjoyed the second verse.

> "If you cannot preach like Peter,
> if you cannot pray like Paul,
> You can tell the love of Jesus and say,
> 'He died for all.'"

We need more Andrews today.

Discussion Questions

1. What was Andrew's action after spending time with Jesus and what can we learn from it?

2. What style of evangelism did Andrew practice and why is this a successful method?

3. What would lead someone to think that Andrew was more thoughtful or withdrawn than Peter, John, and James, the other three of the group closest to Jesus, and how does this relate to many in the church today?

4. How does Andrew show the value of individuals?

5. What gift(s) do you possess and how can you use these in service to our Lord?

4
James and John
Sons of Thunder

As we progress through the list of the apostles, we begin to see less of them mentioned directly in Scripture. This should not cause us to discount their contributions or lessen what we can learn from them. We will continue our study of the apostles by looking at James and John, the other set of brothers called by Christ.

Although given the nickname that leads you to believe these were contentious men, we see later in life that Jesus took those characteristics that led to their nickname "Sons of Thunder" and turned them into humble and faithful followers. This continues to show us that God can use us to His glory no matter where or who we are. We must turn ourselves over to Him. These men did not follow Jesus because they had nothing else to do. They, like the other apostles, were willing to leave everything because of their conviction of who Jesus was.

In this lesson we will look at information about James and John collectively and then individually. We will look at what we can learn from these two faithful followers of Jesus. Let us begin by looking at what Scriptures shows us about these two brothers.

Biblical Information

James and John were the sons of Zebedee, a successful fisherman (Matthew 4:20-22). They were the third and fourth disciples called. Their calling is recorded in Matthew, Mark, and Luke. Although not attributed to them specifically, they would be a natural fit to work with their fishing partners Peter and Andrew as Jesus called them to become, "fishers of men" (Matthew 4:19).

In Mark 3:17 Jesus gave them the nickname, "Boanerges" or "Sons of Thunder," which is apparently a reference to their bold and aggressive personalities. It may have been because they asked Jesus to let them bring down fire from heaven to destroy a Samaritan village that rejected them. (Luke 9:51-56). They also had their mother ask Jesus for special positions in His Kingdom (Matthew 20:20-28; Mark 10:35-45).

We also see them listed in the first grouping of the apostles, indicating they were part of the inner circle closest to Jesus, and, along with Peter, James and John were with Christ at special times (Mark 5:37 [Dead girl]; Matthew 17:1 [Transfiguration]; Mark 13:3 [Mount of Olives]; Mark 14:33 [Garden of Gethsemane]).

Concerning their deaths, James was the first apostle killed (Acts 12:1-2) and the only one, other than Judas Iscariot, whose manner of death we know for certain. King Herod, in an apparent attempt to gain favor with the Jews, and perhaps the Romans, had James killed, "by the sword," indicating a Roman style of execution. John was the only apostle not killed but was persecuted and banished to the island of Patmos where he wrote the book of Revelation.

Compared to his brother John, and to Peter, there is not a lot of information James in Scripture, but we can still learn from James.

We learn to use our passion and zeal to serve Jesus. The word "zeal" indicates enthusiasm to pursue or fulfill a goal or desire. James was a man of zeal and passion, adding further explanation why Jesus gave the two brothers the nickname, "Sons of Thunder." Frequently James was misguided in his actions but remained faithful to Christ.

Another lesson from James is to keep the faith, no matter what the challenge. Historians believe that the death of James occurred approximately fourteen years after the ascension of Jesus. Some believe that Herod killed James because he was recognized as a leader in the Christian community. This indicates that because he let God direct his life, he turned his life, although relatively short, into a wonderful and powerful instrument God could use. James, along with the others, began at Pentecost to proclaim Christ to all with whom he came into contact.

The direct lesson for us is that whatever our characteristics or gifts, when we dedicate them to our Lord's service, we accomplish great things for His glory.

Highlights of John

John is among the most known of the apostles and essential to our knowledge of Jesus, the apostles, and the carrying out of our Lord's will. Here are some highlights from John's life and ministry.

- John is noted for not referring to himself in the first person and was known as, "the disciple whom Jesus loved." This is in direct contrast to a "Son of Thunder."

- John was apparently known to the high priest. We see this as he is a witness to the early trial of Jesus before the Sanhedrin (John 18:15 -17).

- In a tender moment at the crucifixion, we see John in the small group at the cross. Jesus entrusts John with the care of his mother (John 19:26-27).

Historians believe that Mary eventually died in Ephesus under the direct care of John.

- When informed of the apparent resurrection of Jesus by Mary Magdalene, John and Peter ran to the tomb. John outran Peter but did not go in until after Peter arrived. John notes that they did not understand Scripture about Jesus rising from the dead, so they returned to their homes (John 20:1-10).

- John is a prolific writer of the New Testament. He is the author of 5 books: Gospel of John, 1st, 2nd, and 3rd John, and Revelation. This is second only to the number of books written by Paul.

- We also see John was active with Peter after the beginning of the church in Acts.

What We Learn from John

John teaches us about humility. We have noted that in his writings, John rarely refers to himself directly. He also records the detail of Jesus washing the disciples' feet. It seems as if he is reminding himself of the importance of humility.

John teaches us about the kind of love Jesus wants us to demonstrate, a self-sacrificing love that focuses on others.

- John is called the "apostle whom Jesus loved."

- He uses the word *love* more than 80 times.

- In 1 John 4:7-8, John teaches us that love is the characteristic of God.

John teaches us the clarity of being a faithful follower of Jesus. He uses a lot of strong contrasts.

- We are walking in the light or in darkness (1 John 1).

- If we are born of God, we do not sin (1 John 3:9).

- We are of God or of the world (1 John 4:4-5).

- If we love we are born of God if we do not love, we are not born of God (1 John 4:7-8).

John teaches us to be confident in our knowledge of salvation (1 John 5:13). We begin with an acceptance that we are saved and progress to where we are confident in it. This is not a haughty, self-righteousness, but humble gratitude that Jesus has indeed saved us.

John also knew that believers still sin, but his concern is with the overall pattern of a person's life. It is faithfulness, not sin which is the dominant principle in a believer's life and that God rewards our faithfulness. (1 John 1:8-10; 2:1).

Conclusion

We have already stated that Scripture describes the death of James in Acts 12:1-2 at the hand of Herod in AD 44. Because of this, there is little information about where he continued to teach. Most traditions have that he was limited to the region of Judea. There is a shrine to James in Santiago de Compostela in northwestern Spain. It is believed that this is where he is buried.

Although we are not given the details of John's death, Jesus indicated that John would not die as did other apostles (John 21:20-25). Many historians believe John died in Ephesus (Modern Turkey) in AD 98, during the reign of Emperor Trajan. There are several traditions about his death. One is that John was arrested in Ephesus where he was tossed into a basin of boiling oil. According to this tradition, he was miraculously delivered from death and was sentenced to exile on the island of Patmos. Another tradition states that John was killed by a group of Jewish men. There is yet another report that he did not die but ascended into heaven like Enoch and Elijah. In any case, there is no scriptural record of his actual death.

The most likely tradition is that John died of old age. He lived out his years caring for Mary, the mother of Jesus, in Ephesus. He journeyed from a "Son of Thunder" to a gentle man who had a peaceful death among those he loved. We do not have any specific indication why, but perhaps it was the reward for a lifetime of faithfulness to Jesus.

God takes us from where we are + leads us to where He wants us to be.

James and John were changed from "Sons of Thunder" to faithful followers of Jesus. They learned to balance their ambitions, zeal and passions with their desire to follow-through with the expectations of Jesus. This is a great lesson for us today. We can look at our lives and change the focus from serving self to serving the Master.

James would have loved, "The Servant Song."

> "Lord, make me a servant, Lord, make me like You;
> For You are a servant, make me one, too.
> Lord, make me a servant, do what You must do
> to make me a servant; make me like You."

John would have loved the words in the third verse of the song; "I'll Be a Friend to Jesus."

> "To all who need a savior, my friend I recommend,
> because he brought salvation, is why I am his friend.
> I'll be a friend to Jesus, my life for him I'll spend;
> I'll be a friend to Jesus, until my years shall end."

We also make special note of the closing words in John's gospel (John 21:25). In this passage we see the quiet love of a true servant of our Lord:

> "Now there are also many other things that Jesus did. Were every one of them to be written, I suppose that the world itself could not contain the books that would be written."

In all things, I give God the glory!

Discussion Questions

1. Summarize what we know about James and John as brothers.

2. How was James killed and what can we learn from this?

3. List some highlights of John's life as an apostle.

4. Why do you think John was reluctant to refer to himself in the first person?

5. What is the greatest lesson you learn from John?

5.
Philip and Nathanael

[handwritten annotations: Philip was a common name. Called Nathanael in John's gospel. (Matthew, Mark, Luke, Acts Called Bartholomew). Nathanel was Phillip's close friend.]

Friends to All

We noted that usually the best way we bring someone to Christ is by our personal relationship with them. We have friends and acquaintances with whom we can be open about our faith. We have seen that already in Andrew and Peter. We will see it again with Philip and Nathanael.

We also have stated before that as we progress through the list of the apostles, we begin to see less mentioned about them directly in Scripture. Yet we still learn from these great men despite their obscurity in Scripture. Let us begin by looking at the biblical accounts of Philip.

The Biblical Accounts of Philip

Philip is the fifth name on the lists of the apostles. He is mentioned in Matthew, Mark, Luke, and Acts but without any details. Although John does not list the apostles as in the other gospels and Acts, He does give us some details about Philip.

Our first introduction to Philip is in John 1:43 when Jesus calls him. Of note is the expression from this passage that Jesus "found Philip." Some have mentioned that this choice of words communicates that Jesus sought him out. This fits with John's statement in John 15:16 where Jesus stated they did not choose Him, but He chose them and appointed them. Jesus very clearly and directly tells Philip, "Follow me."

John also states that Philip was from Bethsaida (vs. 44), the home of Andrew and Peter, indicating that they likely knew each other, and that Phillip worked as a fisherman. Philip then immediately informs his friend Nathanael about Jesus (we will look more at this later). When Nathanael hesitated in his belief, Philip responds by continuing to encourage him stating, "Come and see" (vs. 46). We do not have the conversation between Jesus and Philip as we do with Nathanael, but thankfully, Philip was persistent in his enthusiasm.

There are other mentions of Philip in Scripture that show his interaction with Jesus.

- John 6:5-6 - Philip is tested by Jesus during the feeding of the 5,000.

- John 12:20-26 - Philip brought 2 Greeks to Andrew. These men wanted to meet Jesus.

- John 14:8 - Philip asked Jesus to show them the Father.

It is not a major point, but some get Philip the apostle and Philip the evangelist mixed up. Philip the apostle was not the Philip in Acts 8. As Acts continues with the narrative of the beginning and growth of the church, we read that persecution of the church had begun. The opening statement in Acts 8 tells us that as the church began to face great persecution, the Christians were scattered, except for the apostles, who remained in Jerusalem. In verse 5, we see that Philip went to Samaria to teach them Christ. Since the Scripture states that Philip the apostle was still in Jerusalem, it must have been the other Philip that we know from Acts 6, one of those chosen to help serve those who had been overlooked.

What We Learn from Philip

Philip teaches us to focus on Jesus and not self.

Like several of the others, Philip had questions and doubts and found it difficult at times to understand even simple

Phillip lacked vision.

concepts but he knew Jesus was the answer to his questions.

All too often we are just like that. We learn that we must be willing to follow Jesus through it all. We might not understand everything, but we know Jesus is the source of our salvation, so we do not give up. Like Philip, we get the answer wrong sometimes, but also like Philip, we continue to learn from Jesus. *Focus on Jesus, not Self.*

Like Andrew, Philip teaches us to bring others to Jesus.

Philip's first action after finding Jesus was to find his friend Nathanael. It was Philip who brought two Greek men to Andrew in order to meet Jesus.

A great lesson for us is that there are times when we do not feel comfortable bringing someone directly to Christ. We learn, however, not to give up or refuse them the opportunity to learn of Jesus. We can bring them to class or worship. We can invite them to a Bible study. We can introduce them to someone who can teach them. The method taught is not nearly as important as the effort of introducing them to Christ.

We have noted that the first thing Phillip did was to go to his friend Nathanael with the good news of his discovery of Jesus. Let us leave Philip for now and look at Nathanael as he encounters his Savior.

There is not much about Nathanael mentioned in Scripture, but he is an important figure in God's plan to teach us several important lessons.

Nathanael

Nathanael is named Bartholomew in Matthew, Mark, Luke, and Acts, but he is called Nathanael in John's gospel. Although some think Nathanael and Bartholomew are different men, given the references and association in the gospels with Phillip and then in John, most scholars think these two are the same man. As such, he is listed as the sixth apostle in the gospels and the seventh in Acts.

John 21:2 states that Nathanael came from Cana in Galilee. He was likely a fisherman since he went with the others to fish after Jesus appears following His resurrection.

Most of what we know of Nathanael is from John 1:43-51 as we read about his calling by Jesus. As we have noted, Philip brought Nathanael to Jesus, but Nathanael was already known by Jesus who previously saw Nathanael sitting under a fig tree. This is not just a passing mention. It was customary for Jews to plant a fig tree by the front of their house. As the tree matured, they would sit under it and study and pray. This adds importance to what Jesus said when he initially spoke with Nathanael.

Jesus identifies Nathanael with a particularly notable statement in John 1:47:

> "Behold, an Israelite indeed, in whom there is no deceit." (Some versions say, "guile").

Rather than say "Jew" or "Hebrew" Jesus said "Israelite." The use of "Israelite" is a religious reference rather than a nationalistic one. It could be interpreted as "Here is a man of God who is honest."

After Nathanael's question about how Jesus knew him, Jesus identifies His knowledge of Nathanael's habit of meditating and praying under the fig tree. Some point to this as the divine power of omniscience (all knowing) of Jesus as part of the Godhead. Nathanael must have thought that because of his response: "Rabbi, you are the Son of God! You are the King of Israel!" *He biblically had a level of knowledge.*

We recall what Philip said when he told Nathanael of Jesus, that Nathanael questioned if anything of merit could come from such a small town. After meeting Jesus, Nathanael went from someone doubting to fully and enthusiastically embracing Jesus as the Messiah.

What We Learn from Nathanael

Nathanael teaches us to *Forget our pride* completely embrace Jesus. *+ embrace Jesus.*

Jesus came to save humanity by reestablishing our relationship with God. More importantly, Jesus came to save each of us individually. It is therefore critical for each of us have a personal relationship with Jesus. That is exactly what Nathanael did; "Rabbi, you are the Son of God! You are the King of Israel."

Like the others, Nathanael teaches us to be a seeker.

As Jesus noted, He saw Nathanael sitting under the fig tree, a place of study, prayer, and meditation.

There are two kinds of seekers, and we see both in Nathanael. From John's record, we see that Nathanael was the first kind of seeker, one who is not sure about the direction of his life and who turns to God, seeking to find that direction. Later, after finding Jesus, he became the second kind of seeker, one who now has discovered direction and meaning through Jesus and seeks to follow His will as a faithful disciple. Nathanael never ceased to be a seeker discovering and following Jesus. *God always answers the seeker. Heb. 11:6 "Without faith, it's impossible to please God."*

Conclusion

God brings the seeker + the savior together.

There is a mix of traditions about Philip's activities as the gospel spread. Tradition states that he traveled throughout Greece, Turkey, and Syria and was eventually killed in the city of Hierapolis because he converted the wife of the proconsul there. It states that he was crucified upside-down. Another tradition of his death states he was beheaded in the city.

Tradition also has that Nathanael carried the gospel to India, Ethiopia, northeast Iran, and Turkey. Most traditions hold that he was killed in Turkey by being flayed with a whip and then beheaded. There is another tradition that states he was crucified upside down like Peter. Some modern scholars believe, but there is a lot of disagreement, that he was more likely to have died in India.

Philip and Nathanael do not seem very impressive when we first see them. Certainly, there is not much in the scriptural record regarding them. However, when we consider their life's work was to serve and glorify the Savior, we see that they are examples of what it means to put ourselves aside and follow Jesus.

We see that Philip and Nathanael were faithful servants of Jesus who had questions and concerns, doubts and fears. Despite these thoughts and feelings, however, they continued to be positive instruments in the hands of God. Once again, through their example we can see that we too can use our gifts to become all that Jesus wants us to become.

I think Philip would have liked the song, "Break Thou the Bread of Life." He would have remembered how Jesus taught him with the fishes and loaves. We see Philip breaking the bread of life to others as he brought them to the Master.

Nathanael would have liked our song "Sweet Hour of Prayer". He would recall his first encounter with the Lord He came to love and serve.

We all need a friend like Philip and his fig tree to lead us to a quiet place of meditation and prayer.

We can use our gifts, whether great or small, to serve Jesus.
In all things we give God the glory.

Discussion Questions

1. Summarize what we know of Philip.

2. How does Philip teach us to focus on Jesus and not self?

3. Summarize how Nathanael was brought to Jesus?

4. In what ways do we see Nathanael as a "seeker" and what can we learn from that?

6.
Matthew and Thomas

Two Men Transformed

Change is possible no matter who it is.

All of us have personal characteristics and traits we do not like. Perhaps these were what drove us to Christ in the first place. Just like Matthew and Thomas, the subjects of this lesson, we can find a change and the grace to continue to grow into what we can be as we turn our lives over to our Savior, Jesus.

Although somewhat obscure compared to some of the others, these two apostles are very well known by many. What we know of Matthew and Thomas for certain is contained in Scripture so that will remain our focus.

Matthew

The information from Scripture about Matthew is straight forward. He is identified as Levi, the Son of Alphaeus (Mark 2:14) and simply as Levi (Luke 5:27). He is universally accepted as the author of the book of Matthew.

The calling of Matthew is recorded in each of the gospels except John. Matthew was a [Jewish] tax collector at Capernaum. There is no indication he had any previous interaction with Jesus, but it is possible that he had heard of Him as the Lord traveled and taught in that region. On the life-changing day of his calling, Matthew was manning his tax booth when Jesus invites the tax collector to follow Him (Matthew 9:9). Jesus is passing by the tax booth and simply says to Matthew, "Follow me." Matthew immediately leaves his booth and follows Jesus.

In Luke 5:27-32, we see the detail of Matthew's actions immediately after Jesus called him. Just like Andrew and Philip, Matthew introduces his friends to Jesus. Matthew puts together a banquet and invites his friends to come meet Jesus. Given his social status as a tax collector, his friends were primarily other tax collectors. The religious leaders saw this as a scandalous event and used it to question the motives and purity of Jesus since he was associating with "tax collectors and sinners." We gain wonderful insight into Jesus and his motives as he responds to the criticism by stating:

> "Those who are well have no need of a physician, but those who are sick. I have not come to call the righteous but sinners to repentance."
> - Luke 5:31-32

We do not have any indication Matthew was dishonest or engaged in questionable practices; however, because of his associations, he would be considered guilty by association. Tax collectors were among the most despised professions in the Jewish society. They were looked at as traitors and collaborators since they served Rome. They were seen as dishonest and unclean because of their association and were a visible target for the hatred the Jews felt towards the Romans.

There were two types of tax collectors. One type collected general taxes such as property, income and poll taxes. These taxes were imposed directly through the Roman government and less subject to graft. The other type collected more arbitrary taxes such as duty on imports and exports, tolls on beasts of burden and axles of vehicles or whatever else they wanted to tax. In addition to the stated tax, they usually added additional amounts that they collected for themselves.

There were also different levels of tax collectors. There were the "chief tax collectors" such as Zacchaeus (Luke 19:1-2) and those that interacted directly with the public, such as Matthew.

Tax collectors were frequently referenced together with prostitutes and other low-level social groups. However, choosing Matthew was consistent with Jesus' method of going to those needing him the most, just as Jesus stated at Matthew's banquet.

Jesus referred to tax collectors on several occasions. One of the best-known references is found in the Parable of the Pharisee and the Tax Collector (Luke 18:10-14). In this parable, Jesus draws a sharp contrast between the self-righteous Pharisee praising himself before God and looking down upon the tax collector standing in the corner. There the tax collector stands penitent before God, not even able to look up to God. He pleads with God for mercy. As Jesus draws the contrast, it is the humble and contrite tax collector who is forgiven and accepted by God. I suspect Matthew hung on every word, fully understanding the emotion of the tax collector in the parable.

In addition to the parable mentioned above, Jesus refers to tax collectors in other settings. We read of Zacchaeus in Luke 19:2-10. Zacchaeus climbs a tree to see Jesus. Jesus spends the afternoon with Zacchaeus, changing his life forever. There is the collective mention in Luke 15:1, Matthew 21:31 and Luke 7:28-29 where Jesus teaches that those at the lowest level of Jewish society were justified and accepted before those seen as righteous. It was not position, acceptance, or rejection by society that saved them, but their level willingness to turn to Jesus.

Matthew was willing to leave all his worldly riches and follow Christ. Matthew put into action the words of Jesus about laying up treasure in heaven (Matthew 6:19-21). Indications are that when Jesus called him, he simply left the money on the table and walked away into a new life.

What We Learn from Matthew

Matthew gives us four "great" lessons: *The sermon is like Kingdom Citizenship 101: The teachings of Jesus.* *The old*

He gives us the detail of the **greatest sermon**, His; Sermon on the Mount (Matthew 5-7). During this sermon, Jesus reveals the simple and direct application of God's expectations of citizens in His Kingdom.

The Present

Matthew gives us what some call the "**Great Commitment**" in Matthew 10:37-39: *We can't sustain our relationship w/ the Lord w/out commitment*

Family was important to Jesus.

> "Whoever loves father or mother more than me is not worthy of me, and whoever loves son or daughter more than me is not worthy of me. And whoever does not take his cross and follow me is not worthy of me. Whoever finds his life will lose it, and whoever loses his life for my sake will find it."

Jesus has to be first.

He also provides us the answer to the question of the "**Great Commandments**" in Matthew 22:36-40:

> "You shall love the Lord your God with all your heart and with all your soul and with all your mind. This is the great and first commandment. And a second is like it: You shall love your neighbor as yourself. On these two commandments depend all the Law and the Prophets."

[handwritten: Show compassion, mercy, & love to our neighbors. The Parable of the Samaritan.]

Matthew records the details of what is referred to as the "**Great Commission**" (Matthew 28:18-20):

[handwritten: Points to the future.]

> "All authority in heaven and on earth has been given to me. Go therefore and make disciples of all nations, baptizing them in the name of the Father and of the Son and of the Holy Spirit, teaching them to observe all that I have commanded you. And behold, I am with you always, to the end of the age."

[handwritten: things of Sermon on the Mount & how to apply them.]

Perhaps Matthew was seeking change in his life when Jesus called him. Matthew could recall that moment and state, "I used to be despised by many, but now I'm loved by the Master." That is a statement echoed by many as we experience the change in our lives as we also encounter our Lord.

In the next apostle, we see a man who also had doubts and misgivings. He was not the only one to doubt, but because he vocalized it, that is how he is known.

Thomas *One of the most known, "the doubter"*

We do not know much about Thomas except his listing among the twelve apostles in the gospels and Acts, and the incidents recorded by John. We do not know his profession, education, or associations.

He is known as Thomas the Twin (John 11:16). Some versions of Scripture use the term "Didymus" which means twin. *in King James*

The first time the gospels record him speaking is in John 11 when Lazarus has recently died, and Jesus wishes to return to Bethany to raise him from the dead. After trying to persuade Jesus not to return, John records:

> "So Thomas, called the Twin, said to his fellow disciples, "Let us also go, that we may die with him." *Remarkable statement of faith + courage.*
> - John 11:16

We read another statement from Thomas in John 14:5-6. Jesus is preparing the apostles for His upcoming torture, death, and eventual return to heaven. Thomas asked Jesus how they could know where He was going. In this event we have another insight into the mission of Jesus stated in John 14:6:

> "I am the way, and the truth, and the life. No one comes to the Father except through me."

All of the Apostles doubted, Thomas just expressed it.

Perhaps unjustly so, but Thomas gained the identity of "Doubting Thomas" because of the incident that happened in John 20:24-29. After the resurrection of Jesus, the apostles were together, except Thomas. We do not know where Thomas was or why he was not with the others. When Thomas arrived, they told him they had seen Jesus risen from the dead. Thomas did not believe them and stated that he had to see and touch the nail marks in His hand and place his hand into Jesus' side before he would believe. Jesus then appears and invites Thomas to do just what he had said. This led to one of the greatest statements of faith in Scripture: Verse 28, "My Lord and My God." From that moment on, Thomas was never a doubter, but a faithful follower into eternity. *"Thomas, great above the faithful." a better way to be known.*

What We Learn from Thomas.

Thomas shows us the Lord forgives.

All the apostles doubted and abandoned the Lord to some degree. As stated, when Jesus appeared to the apostles and invited Thomas to touch Him, Thomas immediately praised Jesus as Lord and God. There was no more doubt of the resurrection of Jesus nor of who He was. Jesus did not condemn Thomas for not believing, rather He blessed Thomas in his belief.

We all go through or have gone through a period of not believing who Jesus is. Some even doubt that Jesus could possibly be what He claims or could possibly forgive them for their sins. Yet Jesus is always ready to forgive those who turn to Him, as seen by Thomas' life. This is a natural process that we all go through.

Thomas teaches us to remain faithful to the Lord.

Our Lord doesn't demand perfection but does demand faithfulness.

Although there were times when his faith was weak, Thomas remained faithful to our Lord. We see in Thomas a willingness to follow Jesus, even in the possibility of losing his life. Therein lies one of the greatest paradoxes, and greatest promises given by Jesus. We must be willing, as He demonstrated, to lay down our life for Him to gain life, also through Him (Matthew 16:25; John 15:13).

Conclusion

Tradition and non-biblical writings record that Matthew carried the gospel to Persia and Ethiopia. Matthew was believed to have died around AD 60 in Ethiopia. Some scholars think Matthew died of natural causes, but most scholars claim he was killed. There are several ways Matthew was believed to have died, including burned, stoned, stabbed, or beheaded.

There is little information about the life and death of Thomas beyond the mentions in scripture. Tradition relates that Thomas carried the gospel to India. It is believed by some that Thomas was killed by being stabbed with a spear. It is possible that this is fictionalized because of Thomas' statement about touching the wound in the side of Jesus (John 20:27).

Matthew and Thomas show us that no matter who we are or what we become, no matter our doubts or fears, Jesus wants us to come home to him. We have learned that they continued to be positive instruments for God. Through their example, we can see that we, too, can use our gifts to become all Jesus wants us to become.

Matthew and Thomas represent two distinct responses to Jesus. Matthew unhesitatingly left his former life and followed Jesus. Thomas followed Jesus but had a notable moment of doubt. Both men are honored because eventually there was no doubt from either of them that Jesus is indeed Lord, Savior and King.

We stated that Matthew gives us four great lessons in his gospel. There is one more lesson Matthew gives, the Lord's **"great invitation"** (Matthew 11:28-30). Here Jesus states:

> "Come to me, all who labor and are heavy laden, and I will give you rest. Take my yoke upon you, and learn from me, for I am gentle and lowly [humble] in

heart, and you will find rest for your souls. <u>For my yoke is easy, and my burden is light."</u> —Because Jesus is carrying it w/ us. Jesus helps us carry that burden.

Matthew and Thomas needed rest. Both learned to trust our Lord and indeed, to take up His yoke.

Matthew would like our song, "Take My Life and Let It Be." He would especially have liked the fourth verse:

> "Take my silver and my gold;
> Not a mite would I withhold.
> Take my intellect and use every power
> as thou shalt choose."

Thomas would love the old gospel song, "He Lives."

> "I serve a risen savior, he's in the world today.
> I know that he is living whatever men may say.
> I see his hand of mercy, I hear his voice of cheer,
> and just the time I need him, he's always near.
> He lives! He lives! Christ Jesus lives today!"

Discussion Questions

1. Summarize biblical information about Matthew.

2. Why were tax collectors despised and how does this fit the type of individual Jesus could use in His ministry?

3. Summarize the "great" lessons Matthew recorded in his gospel and why these are important to us.

4. Summarize why Thomas is referred to by so many as "Doubting Thomas" and what is the true nature of Thomas?

5. What can we learn from Thomas?

6. What lesson do you take away from the life of Matthew and Thomas?

7.
James the Less, Simon the Zealot, and Judas Not Iscariot
Faces in the Crowd

Once I attended a professional basketball game at an arena that held more than 10,000 fans. As I looked around, it occurred to me that, except for my friend sitting next to me, no one in this mass of humanity knew, or cared who I was.

There may have been a time when there were hundreds, maybe thousands around you, yet no one was noticing you. Perhaps you have seen others recognized for great things or promoted to higher levels of responsibility and wished you also could receive such recognition. This might have been the feelings of the three men in this lesson at some point in their discipleship (Mark 10:35-41). Yet, as we study them, we realize that this likely never crossed their minds.

Not everyone can be recognized as a champion. Not everyone will receive acclaim for his or her deeds. But in the Kingdom of God, we receive our crown of glory by honoring the Lord and showing Him to others. That is what marks these three men. They might be seen as obscure and ordinary, among the people in this world, yet they are shining stars in the Kingdom.

These three men represent all the "silent saints" serving our Lord faithfully in obscurity. We may not know of their service, but our Lord knows. They are the ones using their talents in silent service as they feed the hungry and give drink to the thirsty, welcome strangers, clothe the naked, and visit the sick and imprisoned (Matthew 25:31-40). Their names will ring out in eternity.

James the Less

[handwritten: A small, quiet man in the background. vs James, the Son of Thunder]

There are two apostles named James. We have studied James, the brother of John, an apostle that was among our Lord's closest disciples. The other James, James the Less, is named in Scripture only in each list of the apostles (Matthew 10:3, Mark 3:18, Luke 6:14-16, and Acts 1:13) and as a secondary figure in Mark 15:40.

He is also known as, "James the Younger" (Mark 15:40). In Matthew's listing he is identified as James, the son of

He lived daily pointing to Jesus.

Alphaeus (Matthew 10:3). Note that Matthew is also referred to as, "Son of Alphaeus" (Mark 2:14). It is possible that these two were brothers. There is no mention in Scripture to distinguish between the two men listed as, "Son of Alphaeus," or to show James's relationship to Matthew. We simply do not know.

The word "less" in the original language often means "little," as in small in stature. It can also mean someone younger in age, or someone less prominent. Some scholars think James received the name based on his lack of influence compared to James, the son of Zebedee. This gives us an image of a man who was probably small in size, young, and quiet who stayed mostly in the background.

There are no other mentions of this James in Scripture. He did not write any books or ask questions of Jesus that were recorded. He received no rebukes or questions from Jesus. But he was there among the twelve. Perhaps a better name for him would be "James the Faithful."

Our next apostle, Simon the Zealot, probably had an interesting relationship with the other apostles, especially Matthew the Tax Collector.

Simon the Zealot

An extremist given to passions.

Simon is named 10th in the listings of the apostles in Luke's gospel and 11th in Matthew and Mark's. Some versions refer to him as "Simon the Canaanite." This is not a reference to

Canaan or the village of Cana but is a form of the Hebrew word meaning; "to be zealous."

Zealots were an extremist group that hated Romans and were dedicated to their over-throw. They also hated anyone, especially Jews, that associated with or assisted the Romans. They were given to violence and considered to be outlaws. They often carried a knife hidden in their clothing for the purpose of assassinating those they considered enemies of Israel. They believed they were doing God's work.

This must have led to interesting conversations with Matthew. At one time Simon would have gladly killed Matthew, and Matthew would likely have identified Simon to Roman authorities. Yet, here both stand as spiritual brothers dedicated to Christ, spreading the Gospel, and worshiping the same Lord! This illustrates the transforming power of Jesus when we let Him rule our lives. Once enemies, now brothers in the Lord.

The last apostle who remained faithful shares a name with the one who betrayed Christ. When we look at his life, we see that he remained faithful and dedicated to Jesus.

Judas (Not Iscariot)

Judas means "Jevohah leads"

We have noted that several of the apostles had multiple names or are called different names in the gospels. This apostle, Judas, is called by three names. He is referred to by John as "Judas, Not Iscariot," apparently to differentiate him from Judas the Betrayer (John 14:22). In Matthew 10:3, the

King James Version of Scripture refers to him as Lebbaeus whose surname was Thaddaeus.

Other than the lists of the apostles in Matthew, Mark, Luke, and Acts, we see only one other mention of Judas Not Iscariot in John 14:22. Jesus is giving more insight into his relationship with those who love and obey him. Judas (Not Iscariot) asks a simple question for clarification:

> "Lord, how is it that you will manifest yourself to us, and not to the world?"

Likely Judas, as with the rest, was asking this from the view of an earthly kingdom. We see a marvelous answer from Jesus:

> "If anyone loves me, he will keep my word; and my Father will love him, and we will come to him and make our home with him." (vs. 23) He will reveal himself to you, if you love God.

What We Learn from These Three Lesser-Known Apostles

As we have seen, there is little mention of these men in Scripture, yet there are lessons we can apply in our service to the Lord.

It's God's power that is seen.
Being a servant of God is not about us.
It's about the Master.

It is all about showing Jesus through our lives. We must always remember that our Lord is the Master, we are the servants. Our singular focus is summed up in our Lord's words in Matthew 22:36-40 as He tells us to *love God with all our heart, soul, and mind and to love our neighbor as ourselves*. These men turned away from self and towards our Lord.

Glory can be found in the ordinary.

These silent saints served quietly in the background, always looking to understand and do as our Lord asked. They serve as a standard for the countless numbers of silent saints, quietly but effectively going about obeying the Lord and bringing others to Him in ways known only to God.

Their greatness is not in theirselves, but is in serving the Lord.

True faith is durable.
Faithfulness is their greatest asset.

While others left our Lord because of the difficulty of His teachings (John 6:66), they, like the other apostles, remained with him. If they had been seeking personal glory and fame, then they, too, would have likely left. We do know that they, like all the apostles had to learn the true nature of Jesus and His mission, but they did learn. They were counted among the number at Pentecost in Acts 2 to proclaim the message of Jesus to the world. Because of their faithfulness, they will be seated with our Lord in judgment upon twelve thrones (Matthew 19:28).

Conclusion

Given that these three more obscure apostles have little mention in scripture, it is understood that there is little about their life beyond the gospels. There are some traditions and legends. James the Less is believed to have carried the gospel into Egypt. There he was believed to have been crucified. Another tradition states that he was stoned to death. Josephus, a Jewish historian, records that he was killed by being pushed from the pinnacle of the temple, beaten, and then stoned to death.

Simon the Zealot is believed to have taken the gospel to the British Isles after the fall of Jerusalem. He was also thought to have carried the gospel to Persia where tradition says he was ultimately killed in Persia for refusing to sacrifice to the sun god.

Tradition says that Judas, not Iscariot, a few years after Pentecost took the Gospel to the region known today as Turkey. There is not much mentioned about his death except that it is believed he was clubbed to death for his faith.

These three are not seen as giants of the faith by our standards. We might say their most distinguishing mark was their obscurity. Yet there they were, counted among the twelve, handpicked by Jesus for a reason, and ever faithful. They allowed our Lord to change their lives and because of that were part of a wonderful group of men who introduced the world to the gospel. Along with the other apostles, their example continues to teach and encourage us to be faithful.

I think these men would have loved our song, "Living for Jesus."

> "Living for Jesus a life that is true,
> striving to please him in all that I do;
> Yielding allegiance, glad hearted and free,
> this is the pathway of blessing for me."

Discussion Questions

1. Summarize biblical information about James the Less.

2. Summarize biblical information about Simon.

3. Describe the zealots and how this would enable Simon to serve faithfully as an apostle, and how this characteristic helps in our role as disciples.

4. Summarize information about Judas (Not Iscariot).

5. How do these men, with little reference in scripture, teach us in our service to Jesus?

8.
Judas Iscariot
A Life Wasted

[Handwritten margin notes: "Judas never grew in his faith. He never gave his heart to the Lord."]

Up to this point, we have focused on the apostles who are indeed worthy of imitation. Sadly, we see one apostle who had every opportunity to enjoy the riches of eternity but wasted that opportunity. He was not the first person to do so, nor the last, but he is perhaps the most tragic example.

Judas Iscariot is remembered for one thing: his betrayal of Christ. He was one of the original twelve chosen by Jesus and given every opportunity and lesson just as the others. Yet he chose to put himself ahead of Jesus. As a result, he is lost for all eternity. As someone once said, Judas was a man who had given his life to Christ but not his heart.

Judas was a common name and means; "Jehovah leads." Because of his betrayal of Jesus, his name will forever be looked upon negatively. He was not from Galilee but from

He is a nonexample of faithful.

Kerioth, a region south of Judea. He was not related by family or profession to any of the others.

We have no record from Scripture of how or when he was called by Jesus. He might have been part of the larger numbers that heard Jesus teach, saw the power of the miracles, and decided to become a disciple. There simply is no record.

Only Peter is mentioned more times in the gospels than Judas[1]. Matthew gives the most details and Mark the least. Luke and John both state that Satan entered Judas (Luke 22:3; John 13:27). John describes Judas as untrustworthy, giving the detail of Judas in charge of their money and sometimes taking from it (John 12:6).

When we put all the references together, we see a man who was part of the original apostles, having the same opportunities to grow spiritually into a faithful servant. The seed of God's word not only fell on hard soil (Matthew 13:1-9), but upon a hostile heart seeking only selfish gain. The soil of Judas' heart was ripe for the evil of Satan's seed.

Some speculate that Judas entered a point of no return in John 12:1-8 when Mary anoints Jesus' feet at Bethany. In this incident, Mary (probably the sister of Martha and Lazarus) uses an expensive ointment to wash the feet of our Lord.

---

1. "Judas: Betrayer or Friend of Jesus?"
(William Klassen, Fortress Press, 1996)

Judas takes offense of the event because of what he feels is a waste of a valuable ointment. John indicates that his offense was from his greed. Jesus tells Judas to leave her alone. Note also that Jesus provides an insight into an event when later we see that the women went to the tomb to prepare His body for final burial (Mark 16:1).

Some feel there is a contradiction between the selection of Judas as an apostle and his betrayal of Jesus. There is no contradiction based on his choice. In Scripture, we see that he made a conscious choice to betray Jesus (Luke 22:48) and that he chose to be a thief giving into the greed in his heart (John 12:6).

Judas' act of betrayal was part of God's sovereign[2] plan (Psalm 41:9, Zechariah 11:12-13, Matthew 20:18 and 26:20-25, Acts 1:16,20). God's plan did not specify Judas was the one who would betray, only that one close to Jesus would betray. Judas did what he did because of the evil in his heart. He gave Satan a foothold through his greed and evil deeds. Sadly, Judas represents too many who are under the continued influence of Satan and not the love of our Lord.

Luke 22:48 Judas made a conscious choice to betray Jesus.

"Satan entered Judas" doesn't mean Satan entered into Judas involuntarily. Judas's heart was receptive & allowed him in

---

2. https://www.learnreligions.com/what-is-gods-sovereignty-700697

Jn 6:70, Jn 17:12
If Judas had gone to the Lord, He would have forgiven him

Judas' Death

After the arrest of Jesus, Judas realized his guilt of betrayal. He became remorseful and sought to return the money (Matthew 27:3-4). The chief priest rejected the money, so Judas went out and took his life. We must remember that Judas was in control of his life, how he lived it, and how it ended.

He turned to self. He did not turn to the Lord. Then he turned to the chief priests.

※ Remorse is not the same as repentance. Judas was sorry for what he had done but he did not turn to our Lord for forgiveness. He turned to the chief priest and elders, showing where his faith lay. Matthew records that he threw down the money and went out and hanged himself (Matthew 27:5). *Be careful whom you turn to. Turn to Jesus.*

We have more detail in Acts 1:18-19 of the ultimate end of Judas. After hanging himself, Judas fell into a field where he burst open, and his internal organs spilled out. There is no contradiction here. Matthew records the method of his death and Acts records what happened to the body. An evil man who suffered a tragic and lonely death made more tragic because of the wasted opportunity to return to our Lord for forgiveness.

Lessons from Judas

Even though we might not think there is anything to learn from Judas, there is value in looking at what was not done.

Judas shows that God has a plan that cannot be overcome.

Even before God created us, He put into place a plan that would redeem us from our sin and bring about reconciliation with Him. He began to reveal that plan in Genesis 3 after Adam and Eve sinned in the garden. At the betrayal and crucifixion, it seemed to all that it was all over, and that Satan had won. But it was God's plan for a pure sacrifice to endure the ugliest of all sins for us. Yet three days later, Jesus proved the glory of God's plan when he conquered death and arose. Gen 3:14-15

It is tragic that Judas had a role in that plan, but the point is, he chose, even seeking the opportunity for his role. God graces us with the ability to choose His way which leads to life, or to reject Him which leads to death. When we sin, we can choose to return to our Lord in repentance and receive forgiveness (1 John 1:5-9)

Judas is a tragic example of lost opportunity.

He was with Jesus all through His ministry and could have asked Him anything. Judas had received the same power to perform healing and other miracles as the other apostles (Matthew 10:1). But Judas failed to learn what Jesus taught and offered.

In the same way, we have every opportunity to accept our Lord on His terms and receive the blessings He offers. Yet many go through life rejecting Jesus and, in that way, spiritually betraying Him. Rather than repeat the sad end of Judas by taking our life, we must submit to Jesus and gain life... again, the choice is ours.

Judas causes each of us to look at our own life.

We are not disciples for Jesus because of personal gain or fame. We are disciples to serve and honor the Master. As Peter stated,

> "Lord, to whom shall we go? You have the words of eternal life, and we have believed, and have come to know, that you are the Holy One of God."
> - John 6:68-69

When we fail, as we so many times do, we must not give up. We must accept our Lord's forgiveness and seek restoration. If Judas had turned to our Lord, he would have gained forgiveness just as others had. Peter received forgiveness after denying Christ (John 21:15-19). The thief on the cross received forgiveness after first mocking Jesus (Matthew 27:44; Luke 23:40-43). Later Paul, after approving of the stoning of Stephen and seeking to persecute Christians, was forgiven, and in fact, he was then put to work in the Lord's service (Acts 9). More to the point, no matter our sin, when we turn to the Lord, we gain forgiveness. That is the lesson Jesus taught in Luke 15 with the three magnificent parables

Never be afraid to come to the Lord.

on forgiveness, especially the Parable of the Prodigal Son (Luke 15:11-32).

Conclusion

There is no song we sing that Judas can sing with us today. He can no longer praise the Lord. He cannot express his love and devotion. He cannot ask for forgiveness; it is too late.

This lesson is purposefully titled, "Judas Iscariot: A Life Wasted" because Judas was in control of his life and chose to waste it rather than allowing our Lord to redeem it. He is an example for us, but not for imitation. Rather, his is a lesson of one who traded the riches of eternity for a fleeting moment of false gain. He heard Jesus when He said to lay up treasure in heaven but ignored this choosing to serve his personal greed and ambition.

Today, we also hear Jesus and see both sides of the story. Equipped with the teachings of the Lord and the examples of the apostles, we must choose wisely and follow the Lord and not do as Judas did wasting his opportunity for eternal life.

Discussion Questions

1. Summarize information about Judas from Scripture and why you feel he was willing to betray Jesus.

2. How do you reconcile that Jesus chose Judas and that Judas chose to betray our Lord?

3. Using Matthew's account of the death of Judas and the reference from Acts 1:18-19, how do you see Judas' death portrayed.

4. We know Judas experienced remorse for his actions. How does this differ from repentance, and what can we apply from this to our relationship with Jesus?

5. How does Judas help us look at our own life as a disciple of Jesus?

9.
Matthias and Paul

Transition to the Future

The Book of Acts serves as a book of transitions. It takes us from the birth, life, ministry, and teachings of Jesus to the beginning and spread of the church. Within this book of transitions, we see another transition as the Holy Spirit guides the apostles to selecting Matthias to replace Judas and later, Jesus appoints Paul to continue carrying the gospel into all the world.

Although not part of the original twelve apostles, these two men were apostles among the first century church who faithfully served our Lord, and in doing so, teach us valuable lessons. As one chapter in the ministry of Jesus ends and another begins, we see that God's Word continues and that He is active in the flow of that plan. Let us begin by looking at the choosing of Matthias and his role in that plan.

Matthias

We learn of Matthias after Jesus had ascended back to heaven (Acts 1:12-26). About 120 disciples, including the remaining 11 apostles gathered in Jerusalem for fellowship and prayer as they waited for events to happen. Peter proposed that another man be chosen to take Judas Iscariot's place among them to maintain their number and ministry (Acts 1). He based his statements on prophecy from Psalm 109:8 and Psalm 69:25.

Peter then offers qualifications for selection: followers of Jesus from John's baptism until the ascension. Matthias and Joseph (Joseph was also called Justus and Barsabbas) were selected as candidates. Scripture does not give us information about them, but based on Peter's stated qualifications and their selection, it is obvious that they had been faithful disciples of Jesus. After praying together, the disciples cast lots to discern who the chosen man would be, and the lot fell on Matthias. Nothing else is stated in Scripture about Matthias.

It is worthy to note a bit about Joseph (also called Justus and Barsabbas), the one not chosen. He had the qualifications Peter put forward. He had demonstrated faith and a servant heart. Further, although not selected, there is no record in Scripture of any hostility or bad feeling because he was not selected. Indications are that he continued to serve in whatever capacity God required of him. Some scholars believe, because of variations in his name that he might be the "Judas called Barsabbas" mentioned in Acts 15:22. If so, we are assured he remained faithful and active in the early church. We all serve in different capacities, and all roles are important to serving the Lord and His church.

Given that this is the only mention of Matthias, it would seem there is little we can learn, but do not discount Matthias' impact. There are insights and lessons to gain even by what is not said.

We learn from Matthias (and Justus) to be faithful.

We clearly see that the two men put forward for decision were first faithful. That is our lesson. We first dedicate our life to Him and commit to faithful living.

Being ready and being faithful are intertwined.

Certainly, none of the disciples thought anyone would need to replace Judas Iscariot. Although the biblical record always states he was the one that betrayed Jesus, it was not known until after he did what he did. Recall that even at the Last Supper, as Jesus stated that one would betray Him, they asked Jesus to identify him. After Jesus' identified him by handing him a piece of the bread and instructing Judas to do what he had to do, they did not understand Judas as the betrayer (John 13:18-29).

None of us knows for certain the future ahead of us, but we must submit our will to God's and be ready to serve as He desires. Our role is to identify our capabilities and dedicate ourselves to making them available for God's service. We might think we know how our Lord wants us to serve, but all too often the opportunity presents itself in ways we least expect.

We also learn that we serve on God's time, not ours.

We can try as we might to move ahead in our service to fit our timetable, or even to seek to delay our submission to Him, but it does not always work out that way. God takes an eternal view and knows the future for us as we do what we can to be ready. Opportunities to serve will always be there, so we need to remain faithful and ready.

Matthias was chosen, but both he and Justus were faithful and ready. The second apostle later chosen was not ready to serve when he was called. Paul had to learn the hard way that God was ready for him.

Paul

NOTE: Paul is referred to as Saul until Acts 13:9. For convenience, I will refer to him as Paul.

Paul is first mentioned in Acts 7:58 and Acts 8:1 during the stoning to death of Stephen. In Acts 9, as the church is persecuted and driven out of Jerusalem, Paul is appointed by the High Priest to travel to Damascus to bring the Christians there to Jerusalem to face further persecution. Paul adds additional details of this in Acts 22.

As he nears Damascus, Paul is struck down and blinded by a bright light and hears a voice calling to him, and the speaker identifies Himself as Jesus. He tells Paul to go into Damascus where he will be told what to do. Meanwhile, Jesus tells Ananias, a faithful Christian in Damascus, to go to Saul and teach him what to do.

A point to note: In Acts 9:11 Jesus states that Saul is praying. We can imagine that he was praying like never before and asking God what he needed to do. The immediate answer to that prayer was that he needed to become a disciple of Jesus. That is exactly what Ananias did. He healed Paul and then taught him what he needed to do for his salvation. Paul responds by immediately being baptized, thus making him a disciple of Jesus. Following this, he spent the rest of his life teaching Jesus and building up the church.

It is an understatement to say we can learn things from Paul. <u>Paul would go on to write thirteen of the twenty-six New Testament books, and untold other writings and letters to the Christians of the early church</u>. Some scholars feel Paul also wrote the book of Hebrews, although we do not know for certain.

What We Learn from Paul

Like the rest of the apostles, Paul was not perfect, but he was faithful.

In a moment of introspection, Paul shares with us his thoughts about his failings (Romans 7:14-25). He relates how he continues to do what he knows not to do and does not do what he knows to do. This giant of faithfulness even refers to himself as a "wretched man." Yet in that moment, as always, Paul points us to Jesus and His power to save us from our sins. Paul also stated in Romans 3:23 that all have sinned; "all" includes himself.

Paul teaches us to strive for God's standard of perfection as seen through the saving blood of Jesus Christ and our baptism (Romans 6:1-10).

Paul shows in this passage, and many others that repentance, baptism, and the saving blood of Jesus are inextricably connected.

Like Peter, Paul teaches us what did not come easily to him: humility.

Paul teaches us that humility is a characteristic of Jesus and one in which we must grow. The expression "knocked off his high horse" would fit Paul. As he traveled to Damascus, he was full of himself and the righteousness in his cause. He was literally knocked down and shown that he was indeed the servant, not the master. Paul would often speak about always keeping himself in check and relying on God's power, not his own as he lived to glorify the Lord (1 Corinthians 9:24-27).

Paul teaches us how to live as citizens in God's Kingdom.

Paul goes beyond teaching us how to become a citizen in God's Kingdom to focusing on how to live as God expects. Throughout Paul's writings, he teaches us to prepare for service to God in this lifetime with the view that what really matters is being prepared for judgment. Paul takes the principles of godly living and teaches us what they look like in real time. We spend a lifetime learning how to apply the teachings of Jesus as Paul instructs us in the New Testament.

Conclusion

As we have noted, there is no mention of Matthias beyond his selection to replace Judas Iscariot. Traditions within the Greek Orthodox church state that after Matthias taught the gospel in the region of Judea, he spread the gospel into Cappadocia and the region of the Caspian Sea. He is also thought to have traveled with the gospel to Ethiopia. There is a tradition that says he was stoned to death in Jerusalem and then beheaded. One other tradition states that he died of old age in Jerusalem. Scripture is silent on Matthias and history offers very little.

Paul we know served our Lord vigorously throughout his lifetime following his conversion. He was a prolific writer, teacher, and defender of the faith and Christians. There is some debate as to how Paul died. We know he endured multiple instances of house arrest and prison. We also know that he recognized his death was eminent as he wrote to Timothy, Titus, and the others (II Timothy 4:6-8). Based on various historical accounts, Paul was apparently beheaded around the same period Peter was crucified (AD 64-66). Beheading would be the form of death due to Paul's Roman citizenship rather than crucifixion since it was against Roman law to execute a Roman citizen by crucifixion.

These two later appointed apostles, Matthias and Paul, give us the overall lesson of preparedness in service to our Lord. The process of preparing for this service begins with our conversion to Christ and continues into eternity. We should always be ready to serve as our Lord needs us. The opportunities are all around us. Paul further teaches us that the service to our Lord is not on our terms, but the Lord's. Paul learned to submit to the Lord, and he teaches us to do so as well.

Matthias would love the song we sing, "Teach Me Lord to Wait."

> "Teach me, Lord to wait down on my knees,
> till in Your own good time You answer my pleas;
> Teach me not to rely on what others do,
> but to wait in prayer for an answer from You."

Paul would sing long and loud the song, "Years I Spent in Vanity". He likely would tremble (as the second verse states) as he remembered his life.

> "By God's Word at last my sin I learned;
> Then I trembled at the law I'd spurned,
> Till my guilty soul imploring turned to Calvary."

Discussion Questions

1. Summarize the selection of Matthias from Acts 1:12-26 to replace Judas and what we can learn from the event.

2. What are some lessons we can learn from Joseph, the disciple not chosen to replace Judas?

3. Summarize the conversion of Saul (Paul) and how this changed his life.

4. List some things we learn from Paul's conversion and life.

10.
Faith

A Matter of Choice

───

Most of us learn through a combination of what we hear and what we see. We hear an explanation and are then given an example. This technique was masterfully used by Jesus and Peter. For example, in Matthew 5, Jesus uses the illustration of salt and light to explain our role as His disciples in showing Him to the world.

Paul also uses it in several places. For example, in Galatians 5 he teaches about not returning to the slavery of the Old Law and against impure living. He illustrates his point by showing the difference between works of the flesh and fruit of the Spirit. He ends by stating that there is no prohibition against the fruit of the Spirit.

In this lesson we will explore a three-part explanation of faith illustrated by some examples. We will further look at an example of faith gained, weakened, and regained and an example of faith misdirected and lost because of poor choices.

Faith Explained

Perhaps the most well-known verse from Scripture about faith is found in Hebrews 11:1,

> "Now faith is the assurance of things hoped for, the conviction of things not seen."

The writer of Hebrews also provides information on the importance of faith in Hebrews 11:6. Here the writer states that without faith, it is impossible to please God. He completes the thought by saying that not only does faith please God, but it is necessary that whoever would draw closer to God must express faith that He exists and that He will reward their efforts to find Him.

There exists within this great chapter on faith, numerous examples from historical figures from the Old Testament that demonstrate a pattern of faith by their actions. These examples are referred to by many as "Heroes of Faith." In keeping with this series of lessons on the apostles, I want to illustrate how they, too, are heroes of faith.

NOTE: The information following is adapted and modified from the book, "Heroes of Faith – A Study of Hebrews 11" (Bill Rasco, 21st Century Christian, 2012).

Illustrating Faith

By their faithful life, the apostles provide for us an illustration of faith. They gained <u>knowledge</u> of God, learned to <u>trust</u> God, and demonstrated <u>obedience</u> to God. Several times Jesus would say, "Oh, you of little faith." This indicated a faith that must grow.

Paul teaches us in Romans 10:17,

> "Faith comes from hearing and hearing through the word of Christ."

The apostles heard the words of Christ as He explained God's will and how to apply that will. From this, they began to go beyond basic knowledge to internalizing what they had heard thus making them more like Christ. Similar to many listed in Hebrews 11, the apostles also had a level of knowledge of God. The apostles likely gained their knowledge from their upbringing, and participation in synagogue activities. However, their level of true knowledge of God had to grow. <u>Knowledge, therefore, is the first element of faith.</u>

Much of what they thought they knew was misunderstood or misapplied. Several times, for example, as Jesus taught during the Sermon on the Mount, He would state "You have heard it said...but I say." Even at the resurrection of Jesus, the apostles still had certain misunderstandings (John 20:9), but they did have basic knowledge to form a foundation upon which they could grow in their faith.

The second element of faith is trust. Trust is often used as a synonym for faith, but it is actually a part of faith. A key point about trust and its relationship to knowledge is that we generally do not trust or have confidence in something about which we have no knowledge. The more we know of something, the more likely we are to trust. As the apostles learned more about Jesus, they began to grow in their trust. Knowledge and trust create a positive cycle of spiritual growth in that the more we know, the more we trust, which continues to lead to more knowledge and greater trust.

The third element of faith, obedience, is also critical. Just as our trust grows with more knowledge, so too does our desire to obey. Obedience grows as we gain more knowledge and trust. We might obey or go along with something or someone, but we are generally reluctant to obey that which we do not trust. Obedience is a mark of spiritual maturity. We begin by accepting our Lord and realizing more about Him. We then progress to developing faith in Him as we gain deeper understanding and trust. Finally, through a lifetime of dedication, we grow to become more and more characterized as Christ-like. We never fully complete that cycle in this life, but we grow in our faithfulness and effectiveness as we obey our Lord's will.

Jesus teaches us that faith must be accompanied by action (Matthew 7:24-27). Also, James tells us that our faith has no value and is even dead unless it leads to action (James 2:22-26).

Except for Judas Iscariot, the apostles became excellent examples of faith, showing this pattern as they continued to focus on our Lord. They grew in knowledge of our Lord as they learned from Him about God's will. They learned to trust our Lord because of their increased knowledge. They were not only willing to obey, but faithfully sought to obey as they fulfilled their mission to carry the gospel to all the world.

We can look at any of the faithful apostles to see examples of this pattern, but Peter shows what many of us experience. We gain faith, our faith weakens, and we regain our faith.

Peter – Faith Gained

Peter began his walk of faith when he was called to serve by Jesus. We read in John 1:41 where Andrew, after spending the day with Jesus went to his brother Simon and exclaimed, "We have found the Messiah." We do not know a specific moment when Peter believed, but as his knowledge and awareness grew, so too did his faith to where he declared his willingness to even die for the Lord (Matthew 26:33-35; Luke 22:31-32).

Peter – Faith Weakened

Peter's faith walk was a journey. Along the way, his faith weakened in an event that set the foundation for changes to his life that remained forever.

In Luke 22:31-34 we see the event where Jesus tells Peter that he will deny Him. Jesus tells Peter that Satan has demanded that he be allowed to test Peter. Peter declares that he will follow Jesus to prison and even to the death. Jesus replies that before the rooster crows three times that day, Peter will deny him. As the narrative continues and Jesus is arrested, Peter, in weakness and fear denies Jesus, just as He had said Peter would.

When Jesus told Peter he would deny Him, He stated something else that likely escaped Peter in the moment. In Luke 22:32, Jesus states that he had prayed that Peter's faith would not fail. Although Peter's faith did weaken, it did not completely fail. We know that after Peter denied Jesus, he went out and wept bitterly in remorse, disappointment, and shame.

Following this, we see Peter, a man who not long before had declared fealty to Jesus in the strongest terms, has now denied Jesus in equally strong terms; and not once, but three times! Yet Peter held on to his faith, weakened but not lost.

Peter – Faith Regained

As we continue to look at Luke 22:32 we see another statement of hope in the second part of the verse.

> "And **when** you have turned again, strengthen your brothers." (Emphasis mine)

Peter's return did not happen quickly, perhaps not because of his lack of desire, but from his possible lack of belief that he could return. Peter's return to faith would require Jesus offering him forgiveness and reinstatement.

The account of Peter regaining his faith begins in John 20. We read of the resurrection of Jesus and how He appeared to various disciples, and the apostles. Mary Magdalene reports to Peter and John that the tomb was empty. They run to the tomb with John arriving first. He stops to look in, but Peter pushes past him and enters the tomb.

In Mark's record of the resurrection of Jesus we gain additional insight into our Lord's desire to allow Peter to return. In Mark 16 we see several of the women going to the tomb to prepare the body for final burial. They find the stone blocking the entrance moved and a young man (angel) sitting in the otherwise empty tomb who makes a wonderful statement in verse 7,

> "But go, tell his disciples **and Peter** that he is going before you to Galilee. There you will see him, just as he told you." (Emphasis mine)

Notice the emphasis, "and Peter"? Our Lord knew Peter would return and was making the way back for him.

Later, the disciples are in a room with the door locked when Jesus appears among them. Note that Peter is not mentioned by name, only included with the disciples. It is almost as if John is showing Peter, having denied Jesus, is not able to act in his usual outward and prominent way. It is as if he is still doubting himself in a weakened faith. Even as Jesus has His interaction with Thomas, who afterwards no longer doubted the risen Jesus, Peter is still not mentioned.

In John 21, we read of Peter regaining his faith. Peter, along with some of the others, return to their fishing. While they are out in the boat, Jesus stands on the shore and tells them to cast their nets on the other side. When they do, they catch so many fish they can hardly pull in the nets. John then recognizes that the man on the shore is Jesus.

This event was not lost on Peter. He likely remembered the event recorded in Luke 5:4-11 when Luke recounts that Jesus told Peter to go out further and put down nets. Peter stated that the group had been working all night without catching fish, but he did as Jesus said, and they caught so many fish that their nets were breaking.

In John's gospel, he tells how Peter, after realizing it was Jesus, quickly put on his clothes and "threw" himself into the water to swim to shore to be with Jesus. (John 21:7)

Jesus then feeds the disciples from some of the fish they caught. After eating, Jesus and Peter seem to take a walk together (John 21:20). During that quiet time, Jesus asks Peter three times if he loved Him. Peter answers two times, "Yes, Lord, you know that I love you." The third time, just as with his denial of Jesus, Peter adds stronger words as he said, "Lord, you know everything; you know that I love you." Using language showing Jesus as the Good Shepherd, Jesus gives Peter a personal commission as the leader of the effort to shepherd our Lord's flock.

There was no doubt in Peter's mind that our Lord asking him three times and then telling Peter to follow Him (verse 19) showed Peter that our Lord has forgiven him for the three times he had denied Him. Now fully restored and redirected, Peter has regained his faith and spends the rest of his life encouraging and strengthening the faith of others.

How wonderful it would be if all who doubted, denied and abandoned our Lord would return. Sadly, one apostle, Judas Iscariot, did not experience the forgiveness available for him.

Judas – Faith Misdirected and Lost

Judas was one of the twelve chosen by Jesus as an apostle and is listed in every listing except Acts 1:13. Of particular interest is the reference to Judas in John 6:70-71. Many of the disciples had turned away from Jesus because what He was teaching was difficult to understand and accept. Jesus states that He had chosen the twelve but that one of them was going to betray him. John specified Judas. But in that moment, Judas continued to follow our Lord.

Judas was with Jesus from the beginning and traveled with Him just as the others had. He had been given the same gifts to drive out demons, and to heal, and the charge to proclaim the good news of Jesus (Matthew 10). Jesus did not hold anything back from Judas. While the other disciples grew to know, trust, and obey Jesus, Judas did not.

Perhaps identifying Judas as His betrayer, Jesus was giving him a chance to abandon his sinful plan (Mark 14:20; John 13:21-27). Note in this interaction, it was not until Jesus finally identified Judas as the betrayer that Satan entered the heart of Judas.

Judas' faith never ripened because he failed to internalize the words of Jesus. The other apostles also had weaknesses to overcome. The difference was that the others chose to return to Jesus when they failed whereas Judas chose to remain apart.

The others fled from Jesus in fear, but they returned. Judas, too, could have returned and would have been forgiven. Instead, after realizing his sin in betraying Jesus, Judas went to the chief priest to find forgiveness. His faith was misdirected towards the priests and not towards Jesus. Judas now had no hope since those in whom he had faith would not and could not offer forgiveness. Judas tragically took his life, a life wasted.

Remember Jesus' words to Peter in Luke 22:31-32,

> "**And when you have turned again** strengthen your brothers." (Emphasis mine)

Imagine the story Judas could have told. Imagine the impact of telling others that even the one who betrayed Jesus found forgiveness, and so can we.

Choose this Day...
Putting Our Faith into Action

A major gift and way in which we are created in the image of God is our ability to choose.

- God chose to create us
- God chose to save us
- We choose to disobey and reject God

- We choose to submit or return to God
- We choose to remain faithful

Choice has consequences, both positive and negative. We must choose wisely as Peter and so many others have done. Peter chose wisely to return to our Lord and was forgiven, whereas Judas chose poorly and turned away without hope. When we choose to follow Jesus, we choose wisely and put our faith into action, coming to know God, trust God, and obey God. Our faith continues to grow and we become more effective as servants of the Father.

Conclusion

Faith brings us to God and keeps us in that relationship as we grow and live as God wishes for us (Hebrews 11:6). Peter developed faith, saw his faith weakened, and regained it. He went on to serve our Lord faithfully, even to death as he said he was willing to do. Judas had a misdirected faith, sometimes in himself, and sometimes in others, but not in our Lord. When his faith was challenged, he lost it.

The events of Peter's denial and Judas's betrayal occurred in the same time frame. They both had choices and consequences. Peter chose wisely by returning to the Lord. Judas chose poorly by not returning to the Lord. Peter came to know God, trust God, and obey God. Judas did not.

In Joshua 24:14-15, Joshua charges Israel to choose whom they will serve, either the gods of their forefathers and those around them, or Jehovah God. He then states that he and his house will serve the Lord.

That is the same choice we have. We can serve the false gods around us which leads to an empty life, void of all hope and ultimate spiritual death, or we can serve our Lord and Savior Jesus Christ which gives hope and leads to a fulfilled and eternal life.

I pray you will make the same choice as Joshua. I also pray for you as Peter prayed in his last recorded words:

> "But grow in the grace and knowledge of our Lord and Savior, Jesus Christ. To him be the glory both now and to the day of eternity. Amen."
> - 2 Peter 3:18

Discussion Questions

1. Explain the interaction of the three elements of faith: Knowing God, Trusting God, Obeying God.

2. How did the apostles demonstrate the three elements of faith in their journey to becoming more faithful and how does this apply to us?

3. Explain how Peter gained, weakened, and regained his faith, and how does this mirror our faith walk?

4. Explain how Judas' faith was misdirected and lost and the warning for us?

5. Explain how the ability to choose is a gift from God and how we should use it to put our faith into action?

Made in the USA
Las Vegas, NV
02 February 2023